Brain Development

The Ultimate Guide to Transforming Your Life By Changing Your Thoughts

I0416965

Table of Contents

Introduction

I want to thank you and congratulate you for downloading the book, **Brain Development**: The Ultimate Guide To Transforming Your Life By Changing Your Thoughts.

This book contains proven steps and strategies on how to radically transform your life by simply changing the way that you think. In many instances the major distinguishing factor between the mediocre and the successful is a difference in thinking.

This is revolutionary news; anyone can become successful!

This may sound too good to be true, but this thought might be a sign that you fall into the mediocre category and not the successful. A radical change in your life can really be the result of a few changes in the way that you think.

What is interesting is that this applies to any area of life. Would you like to be more successful financially? Would you like to be more successful romantically? Would you like to be more successful socially?

The single determining factor in Success is the way that you think.

Anyone can change the way they think. Will you become everything that you want to become over night? Probably not. But for the cost of a cup of coffee you will be well on your way, and the irony is that it's the only road to get where you want to go.

Thanks again for downloading this book, I hope you enjoy it!

Chapter 1

Personal Responsibility: Throw Away the List of Excuses

Some of the first words that a child learns are, "That's not fair!" Followed closely by, "I didn't do it." From an early age we understand the benefit and convenience of removing the blame from ourselves and placing it squarely onto someone or something else. The problem is that most of us are never corrected and cultivate this habit well into our adult lives.

Many of us are so good at this skill that we can craft excuses for just about anything. To be successful you must be willing to stand up and say "I am responsible for how my life turns out." It is a sure sign of maturity when you can say that your past and your future are your responsibility alone. It's not my parents fault, it's not the governments fault, and it's not the economy's fault. It's not because of where I grew up, it's not the color of my skin, and it's not because prices are too high. It's not that these things aren't true, or that they aren't real. The point is that none of these excuses will help you achieve any of your goals.

In fact, excuses are what keep most people from achieving what they want.

Being responsible and owning up to your life, the good and the bad, is the first step on the road to success. Outlined below are few of the reasons why we should take personal responsibility:

Taking responsibility helps other people like and respect you.

Nobody likes a complainer. You can be excellent in almost every area of your life, but if you complain (which is another form of an excuse) no one is going to want to be around you. Most of us can't live our lives without working with and around other people, and it is beneficial when these people like us and want to work with us. There are so many people peddling their list of excuses that when someone meets a person who accepts responsibility for their lives it is refreshing. They are intrigued and want to know your secret. Whatever your goal is, having people like and respect you will only help.

Accepting the consequences for your actions helps you learn from your mistakes.

Trial and error is a very valuable tool. Excuses keep you from seeing and addressing the errors, because they are disguised as someone else's problem. When you accept personal responsibility for your life, and are fully invested, you are then able to learn valuable lessons from your mistakes. This will then teach you not to repeat the same mistakes, and in turn help you make smarter decisions. Personal experience can be painful, but it's an excellent teacher.

Identifying the excuses will show you the real issues. I use to have a laundry list of "reasons" for why my life wasn't turning out how I wanted it to. I would whip this list out anytime I failed to accomplish whatever I attempted. It's great to have a list of excuses, because you can never fail. The problem with having a list of excuses is that you can never achieve either. I will never forget the day that I learned that everyone has a list of excuses. The difference is that the successful people have thrown away their list and started working while the rest of us keep reading ours aloud to anyone who will listen.

There are times when there are legitimate hurdles that we must overcome to achieve our goals. We will learn how to deal with those later. However, most of our excuses are not legitimate hurdles but excuses used to deflect responsibility. There is no use in lying to ourselves any longer. It's not time to save face or pride; it's time to get to work on our goals and dreams. How can you tell the difference between an excuse and a legitimate hurdle? A good method of distinguishing between the two is to write down each one and ask yourself this question, "Can I change this?" or "Can this be changed?" If the answer to either of these questions is no, then cross out the excuse.

Remember: Personal responsibility is accepting the consequences for your actions instead of blaming others for them. It means getting rid of your usual excuses and owning up to your mistakes. By making a habit of taking personal responsibility for your actions, you no longer waste energy on the things you can't change, and you can now focus on the real hurdles that must be overcome to accomplish your goals. There's no benefit in kidding yourself any longer. If you are overweight it's time to step on the scale and see what needs to be addressed. If you are in debt, it's time to tally up your liabilities and see just how deep the hole is, so you can start to climb your way out. If you are lazy and behind in life, it's time to take inventory and see where you need to focus your attention. Excuses cloud the playing field and keep you from seeing reality. Only give attention to the things in your life that are under your control, and forget about the rest.

Chapter 2

Recognize and Eradicate Your Poor Thinking Habits

James Allen once said, "He thinks in secret and it comes to pass, environment is but his looking glass." Thoughts are a powerful thing, but most of us wield them haphazardly. By the time we are young adults our minds and personalities are shaped to a great degree. Our thinking becomes habit and routine, like a river, and our thoughts must follow wherever the ravine takes us. As our negative thinking takes over our mind like strangling vines, the years continue to pass and we lose our goals and dreams. We form perceptions of reality and assume that everyone else thinks and sees the world as we do. They do not. An interesting fact is that your perception of reality is almost always *wrong.* The good and bad news is that our lives are most affected by the way we *think* things are, *not* the way they actually are.   Be careful what you think about, it absolutely will shape your life.

The first step is finding out where our thoughts have gone wrong, and removing them from our mind. Many times these thoughts are so in grained in us that they have shaped our self-image.

The woman grew up overweight and was constantly ridiculed. She believed these things were true and eventually her thoughts made her identify "The Fat Girl." These thoughts now keep her from achieving her goal of lean body. She can't lose weight because in her mind she is "The Fat Girl." It's the way it's always been and she assumes it must always be this way.

The same process occurs with the guy who has been the jokester since he was a child. Those around him reinforced this image and a daily habitual thought pattern identifying himself as the clown, has kept him from achieving his academic or financial goals. He can't get good grades because he's "The Clown." He can't achieve financial success, because he's "The Clown." It's the way it's always been and he assumes it must always be this way. It would be inconsistent with his self-image if he acted otherwise.

This process can play out in a thousand different ways and circumstances. But the root of the problem is the same in every scenario. The problem is with poor thinking habits. Your current circumstances are the product of your daily thoughts. Let that sink in for a moment. You are where you are, and have what you have, because of the thoughts that you've had daily. You could have had thoughts that would have changed your life and made a different outcome. Everything exists in the mind before it exists in the world. Therefore, the only difference between the billionaire in his mansion and the homeless man on the street are the thoughts in his mind. For the nerds among us, we could demonstrate this in a simple equation.

Circumstances= Thoughts X Time

Here we will be focusing on our mental gardening so to speak. We need to pull some weeds. Many of our poor thinking habits are having devastating effects on our lives, and they are keeping you from becoming the person you desire to be:

Silence the negative self-talk

Most of us our inundated with negative self-talk on a daily basis. It's a wonder that we can achieve anything at all.

It's like we've created our very own personal failure coach that lives in our minds and conditions us to fail at everything that we try. This voice needs to be silenced.

There is a useful exercise that can help us with our negative self-talk. This is not new and there are varying lengths to this exercise. Here we shall call it the 21 day Thought Cleanse Diet. For the next 21 days, I want you to be aware and cognizant of your thoughts throughout the day. Anytime you feel a negative thought, I want you to immediately replace it with a positive thought or solution. For example: You know you need to go to the gym, and as you start the process, you are immediately assailed by a barrage of negative thoughts. As soon as the first thought enters your mind, I want you to immediately reframe it. It will look something like this.

"You will never be in good shape, because you've always been fat and you always will be fat."

Response: "No, what I meant was that I have made poor choices in the past but I am a strong, motivated individual. I can and will change my body."

The goal here is not to have absolutely no negative thoughts. That's not possible, at least not at first. The goal here is to replace those thoughts as quickly as possible, almost as if you aren't letting them take root.

Also, if you are unable or forget to replace the negative thought with a positive thought, you have to start over on day 1. So if you allow negative thoughts to remain without being replaced on day 13, you must start back over at day 1. It sounds silly but this exercise can absolutely transform your thought life. Just give it a try, commit to three weeks. After 21 days you can decide for yourself. Your thoughts are powerful. You need to be able to control and use them for your purposes.

Remember: Your thoughts have an incredible effects on your life. Be intentional about them, and be intentional about removing negative thoughts. The negative thoughts will do their damage no matter the source, so be on your guard. Remove the sources of negative thoughts in your life. Sometimes this means limiting interaction with those people that suck the positivity from your life. This could also mean passing on the nightly news with all of the stories about murder, rape, and natural disasters. It absolutely affects your mind. Find the weeds and remove them from your garden. This is vitally important to your life and wellbeing.

Stop dwelling on past mistakes

One of the main differences between a champion athlete and the average person is the time it takes them to recover from a loss. Successful people do not dwell on failure. When the guy with poor thinking habits loses on the court, he rehearses and dwells on his mistakes. He defines himself as his failure, and it could take days or longer for him to recover and feel confident again.

When the successful individual loses he quickly removes it from his mind. He learns from his mistakes but quickly wipes the slate clean. While the poor thinker says, "I'll never win, look at my failure," the successful person says, "I'll get you tomorrow, just wait." It's almost like water rolling off of a ducks back. Mistakes can be a good thing; they teach us how to succeed. We have to see them for what they are. We learn and keep moving towards our goal. Remember it's the *next* opportunity that matters, not the last.

Throw away the script

Like we have discussed previously, much of our minds and personalities are shaped from an early age. By young adulthood we have a significant self-image that we identify with as a person. The example given before was about the girl who grew up overweight. People around her reinforced this image in her mind, and now she sees herself as "The fat girl." I like to call this self -image our "script." Many times this negative or limiting self-image can be devastating to our goals and futures. We can't achieve what we want because it isn't in line with the script we have or how other people know us.

Maybe the quiet introvert wants to be the funny, charismatic, life of the party. Or your goals would require an individual like that. However, your "script" says that you are the quiet serious guy. You've always been the quiet serious guy. No one knows you as the funny, sociable person. There becomes the compulsion to keep everyone's view of us consistent. We feel that we have to play the part. What would they think of me if I started being confident, funny, and sociable?

Throw away the script. You don't' have to be the person you've always been. And If you haven't been successful, you don't' want to be the person you've always been.

Stop playing by everyone else's rules, because they are definitely not going to play by yours. It may be uncomfortable in the beginning, but it will be well worth it in the end. When you feel that disconnect between how you want to be and that self or script that everyone knows you as, you must push through. We will finish with a quote from William James, "To change one's life: Start immediately. Do it flamboyantly."

Remember: It is vital that we monitor our inner conversations. The overwhelming majority of these conversations are negative, and they have a tremendous effect on our lives. You don't have to be who or what you have been. You can throw away the script at any time and make a new one. If you decide to, you can revolutionize every aspect of your life. You don't have to be the same from this day forward.

Chapter 3

Cultivate the Disciplines of Success

In the last chapter we discussed removing the poor thinking habits from our minds. In this chapter we will discuss cultivating the positive disciplines that are required for success. I would like to define our term for a moment. We see the word discipline and immediately think of work. Well it is work, but I think there could be a more helpful way to define it. Discipline refers to the work required to get where you want to go. It's not this stand alone, ambiguous term that means "work". It's not this high virtue that is optional for only the hardest working people. We need to realize that discipline is only describing the road that leads to our goal. So when we see this word discipline, from now on I want you to imagine the path that takes you from where you are, to where you want to be. There is no other way.

Now we all know and admire discipline when we see it. The disciplines required will change with the varying goals and dreams. Of course getting six pack abs will not require the same disciplines as wanting to become successful financially. Here I want to outline some major disciplines that can be transferred across the board to just about any goal or desire you have. Many of these are tried and true, and many successful people acclaim their merits.

Lastly, we are always looking outside for the path to success, or how to overcome this, or how change that. It was revolutionary for me to learn that what needed to change was not my circumstances. What needed to change was *Me*. A favorite quote of mine from Jim Rohn goes like this, "If you will change, everything will change for you." Personal development is a lifelong process, and it is required if you want to change your life.

A good illustration of this is one that Mr. Rohn uses when he talks about our personal philosophy. He says that our personal philosophy is like the set of our sail, and we are a boat. We can't change the winds, and we can't change the waves. The only thing that the boat can do is change the set of its sail. We can change this sail by changing our life philosophy. This change is produced through the process called personal development. Personal development is a lifelong process and a priority for anyone who wants to become successful.

It's all well and good to talk about philosophy and success, but talk is useless if we don't roll up our sleeves and get to work. Implement these practices into your life and you will be well on your way to transforming your life:

Read the books

Reading is absolutely fundamental to changing who you are and becoming who you want to be. This applies to all areas of life. A good way to get a feel on whether someone is serious about success is by taking a look at their library. What sort of books are you reading? Is reading books a discipline in your life? It's time to make reading a fixture in your life.

It has been said that the only difference between you now, and you 5 years from now, are the people you meet and the books you read. Reading is vital to our growth, and absolutely necessary for our success. You will be hard pressed to find a successful individual who does not read. It is a unifying thread in successful people across all fields of industry.

We saw earlier that we can't change circumstance, but we can change ourselves. The only way to change your life is to change your mind and philosophy through reading. The amazing thing is that resources are more plentiful now than ever before. If there is something you want to do, someone has written a book on how to do it. Do you want to lose weight? There are men and women who have lost weight and wrote it down in a book. Do you want to start a successful company? There are men and women who have created financial empires and written it down in books. Do you want to become a better manager? There are books written by the best managers in the world.

Now, if we have access to books that will teach us just about anything we want to learn, why do we not read them? How could you explain that? Before you answer that question, remember Chapter 1, and throw away the list of excuses. If success is that important to you, you will bypass the present pleasure for tomorrow's fortune. Instead of watching an hour of television before you go to sleep, read a book. If you have an extra 30 minutes to scroll Facebook on your lunch break, grab a book. Invest in yourself. Put in the time and read.

Whatever you want to achieve, there is a book written by an individual who has achieved. Become a student. Get serious about changing who you are. Get serious about achieving your goals.

Exercise: I want you to think of your highest priority goal and find a book on the topic (If you don't have any goals, come back after the next section). It could be finding a spouse, learning how to be confident, or starting your own business. Set aside at least 15 minutes per day until you finish the book.

Remember: Set out to make reading a habit in your life. You don't' have to read a book per week; you can start small. Just start reading. If you will commit to making reading an intentional and habitual endeavor in your life, you will be absolutely amazed by the transformation in your life.

Set your goals

If you asked the average person "What are your short and long term life goals," they would probably look at you like you were an alien. If they did answer the question, it may be something vague like, "I want to be successful."

That's not really their goal, that's just what they hope happens by accident. Goals are used by many successful people, and just by setting goals you are inducted into the top 5% of people. That's right, less than 5% of people have written out and well defined goals. Goals are vital to success and we will discuss some methods for setting goals and their benefits.

I want you to take a sheet of paper (Typing a word document is not the same) and number 1-50. Fill in each line with a goal. Be very specific about your goals, and put everything on the list. Be as detailed as you possibly can. If your goal is a home, include the square footage and describe how it looks. Do this with each entry. If a goal of yours is to eat at a certain restaurant or have a certain type of dog put it on the list. You probably haven't thought about these things before so it may take some thinking. Don't let your mind limit you here. Pretend that there are no limitations. If you make $30,000 a year currently and you want to make $500,000 per year, put it on the list. Don't let your circumstances define your dreams or goals. The greater the goal, the greater the pull on your life. Any of your goals are achievable. It's not going to be easy, but it is absolutely possible. Spend 5 minutes on this exercise.

Now go through your list and put a number next to each of your goals. The number will be the amount of time you think it will require to reach that goal. The house may require 10 years, however, the goal of losing 25 lbs.

might take a year. It may take 5 years for you to be able to visit Paris. If you don't know, just make a guess. Label each of your goals with a 1, 3,5, or 10 now.

Goals are important because they create a future for you. Let's think about this for a moment. The difference between the average Joe shooting the basketball at the gym and the NBA MVP is a difference of goals.

Your goals pull you into the future. The pull of your future needs to be stronger than the pull of your past. This is something that successful people utilize when they are achieving their goals. The person with goals walks differently, talks differently and has a different handshake. They are living life on purpose.

To be able to pull out this list and visualize that home or car or way of life that you desire, has an incredible power. The person without goals is a reactor in the stage of life. He is simply reacting to circumstances and hoping that things will turn out ok in the end.

We have to remember that things won't turn out how we want by accident. Based on our past we see that things might actually get worse. Just hoping for the best hasn't worked for us thus far. The good news is that it can get better, but it's up to us to change it.

We wouldn't start building a house without blue prints and knowing exactly what we are trying to create. Yet, we do not design a future for our own lives. We are like the mason who is laying bricks, and someone walks by and asks "What are you building?" He responds, "I don't know, but I hope it turns out to be a success." That guy wouldn't have a job for much longer. This is our life; we have to think better about these things. It's time to wake up and plan the future that we desire. We must design our future, and if we will make our goals strong enough they will pull us into the future like a magnet.

One of the reasons why goals are so important to your success is because of an incredible mechanism in your brain called the "*Reticular Activating System*." This phenomenon is also why affirmations are a great tool for your success. (We will learn about these in the next section) There are more intelligent people that can describe the scientific and neurological processes in grand detail but I will give you the condensed version.

 An easy way to demonstrate this phenomenon is to think about a time when you bought a new car. You're driving down the road enjoying the new car smell, and you can't help but notice there's another car exactly like yours. You drive a little further and there is another one. You look to the left and there is one at the gas station. You start to feel like everyone has the same car as you!

 This system provides a link between your conscious mind and your subconscious mind. You can actually program this system by setting goals and saying affirmations. This system cannot tell the difference between reality and fantasy, so the process is simple. When we design this grand future for our lives this system finds a way to make it come to pass. I like to think of it like your GPS system in the car. What happens when you make the wrong turn? The system says, "Recalculating...." It is constantly finding the way to get to your predetermined destination. This mechanism helps us tweak and adjust as we are pursuing our dreams. The mind is an incredible machine; use it to your advantage.

Track your progress

Along with this idea of setting goals is the corresponding discipline of tracking your progress. When was the last time you took inventory of your life? Hopefully this book is knocking loose the cobwebs and opening doors in your mind that have been closed for a long time.

Along the journey to your goal you need to have progress reports. A company wouldn't go months without looking at the accounting ledgers and neither should you. Are you making progress towards your goals? Another benefit of tracking your progress is that as you are moving forward you may realize you need to increase the intensity to reach your goals. It allows you to divide your goal by time and figure out what exactly you need to do every day to achieve your goal. Don't let too much time pass between checking you progress. There are a few key periods to check your time. These include: Daily, weekly, monthly, and yearly. Was today a success? There's an old saying that has really helped me break my large goals into manageable chunks.

"Win the day, and you will win the war."

Everyday remember that you just need to make that day a success. Don't worry about the long term today, all you can do is make today a win and you will make the year a win. Make this your mantra and you can achieve anything that you set your mind to.

Go to bed early

I won't bore you with scientific facts about how much your body needs sleep but I do think that this bears mentioning. Most of us are running on fumes and have horrible health. We wonder why we don't' ever feel good. It's difficult to achieve your goals and dreams when you feel fantastic, and it's nearly impossible when you feel bad or tired habitually. Make going to bed early a priority. Try to get at least 8 hours of sleep every night.

Also, don't watch television or surf on your cell phone at night before you go to sleep. The bright light against the dark backdrop of your room actually makes your mind stay awake longer. This effect makes it more difficult for you to go to sleep and get a good night's rest.

Remember, if you feel good you're going to be better at everything you do.

Wake up earlier

If you usually have to get up at 7 am for work, set your alarm for 6 am. I have found that the earlier your get up, the better the result.

 This discipline serves two purposes. First, it changes the whole psychological dynamic of waking up for the day. Instead of "I have to get up for work," you change the dynamic to "I am getting up to accomplish my goals." You are no longer reacting to your life, but you are intentional and focused. You are in control. You choose to wake up and get started. It adds a power and vigor to your mind and body.

 Secondly, you should take this extra time to enjoy your morning. Spend time reading, and looking over your goals. This also allows you to plan out your day, without rushing around so that you aren't late for wherever you need to be. The idea here is an overall shift in attitude. You are in control; you are running your life.

Affirmations- An affirmation is simply a statement that declares something to be true. Many successful individuals have used affirmations to create the life of their dreams. I find the affirmations spoken aloud in the early morning have an incredible impact and set the tone for the rest of the day.

In the earlier chapter we learned about the Reticular Activating System and how we can use utilize affirmations to achieve our goals. Here a few examples affirmations that you can use as examples. You will want to tailor your affirmations to your specific goals:

- I am the owner of a successful graphic design company; I am strong, competent, and financially independent.

- I am worthy of achieving my dreams and I am successful with everything that I touch.

- I will quit smoking with ease and joy, and I will remember that being healthy is more important than pleasure.

- I am walking across the stage to accept my master's degree, and I am proud of my achievement.

- I am driving my beautiful new Maserati along the highway, and I am proud of what my hard work has produced.

Make time to exercise

As you probably well know, exercise has myriad benefits for the mind and the body. It creates a healthier body and reduces physical and mental stress. Once again, it is a lot easier to work on your well designed life when you feel good. The ancient philosophers propounded the effects of good health. Anyone who is chronically ill can attest to how miserable life can be in that state. Most of us take feeling good for granted.

Your current activity level and health will determine what sort of exercise you should be doing. The goal here is to be pushing yourself out of your comfort zone. Exercise, like reading, is meant stretch and make you become a little more than you were before. If it's easy and undemanding then it's not doing you much good. With saying that, your fitness level may require that you start small. You may need to start with a light walk. If that's where you are right now than that's just fine. Don't overdo it. I find that exercising in the morning sets a great tone for the rest of the day, but do what works for you.

This is going to be difficult in the beginning, but after a while you will start to enjoy and look forward to this time. The benefits will be extraordinary.

Adjust the diet

 Diet is another vital component of your overall health. Moderation is the key, and that's why it's been a virtue since the dawn of time.

We all know what is healthy and yet we choose not to eat that way either out of laziness or complacency, or both. Whatever it takes to get you to eat healthier you should do it. It's difficult to achieve your goals and dreams if you don't feel good. And if you do achieve them, it's difficult to enjoy them in poor health. Take the time to read the books on nutrition, and get healthy. You only get one body; you shouldn't hate living in it. Being healthy and fit not only does wonders on your body, it has amazing physiological effects. There are many people whose total personality changes after they get healthy because they didn't realize that their poor health was making them miserable.

Take the time to make this area right, it's important. My personal philosophy in this area is that you should try to eat healthy foods about 80% of the time and reduce the overall size of your meals.

Learn to deny yourself

In the modern western world self-denial is a foreign concept. We get what we want and we get it now. Ancient philosophers as well as theologians knew the benefits of such a discipline. We aren't ever taught that willpower is something that you train, much like a bicep or a hamstring. It's a difficult process, but its well worth the results. We should desire to hone our minds and to have a strong will. I don't think it's a stretch to say that we generally have weaker minds than our ancestors. The sorts of circumstances and trials that they endured would destroy many of us. Our willpower has been gorged and as a result it's obese and non-responsive. Take the time and effort required to strengthen your will power.

If there is something you desire or want, make denying yourself a challenge. It can be as simple as a cupcake, or wanting to buy a new pair of jeans. Every now and then abstain from an activity that you desire. This has the benefit of strengthening your mind and willpower but also creating an incredible confidence in knowing that you are capable of such discipline. Work your willpower muscle, and in the process create a honed mind with a steel resolve. It is this mental strength that helps the man or woman push through any obstacle that stands between them and their goals. You will need it along your journey towards your goals.

Create an invincible confidence

An important aspect of the successful mind is a confidence that cannot be diminished. Most of the successful people in the world have this kind of self-confidence.

 What I don't mean here is an ego that defies all reason. What I do mean, is a confidence that believes that you are capable of achieving your goals. There seems to be an almost delusional aspect to this confidence. These people always believe in the best case scenario, and they realize that the greatest power they can wield is to believe that they can achieve whatever they set out to achieve. They believe that against any odds they can achieve what they set out to do. It's that idea that if you get knocked down 7 times you will get up 8. The possibility that they might not achieve never enters their mind.

Remember: What I don't mean here is mere positive thinking. What I am talking about is an intense confidence coupled with desire and purpose. This is a change in belief, a change in your perception of the world. Perception determines the outcome of your life more than anything. It's not how things are, but how you *think* things are that determines the outcome. The optimist says the glass is half full, the pessimist says the glass if half empty. How could the same measure have two different effects on someone? It is all in your perception. Henry Ford profoundly said, "Whether you think you can, or you think you can't—you're right. Believe that you can achieve your dreams, there is no other way.

Chapter 4

Enough!: The Day You Decide to Change

There comes a point in your life when something happens or you have a realization, and it sets your life on a new path. From that day on you are able to look back and say, "That day was the day that I decided that I'd had enough." There are many successful people who can attest to this experience.

You need to get the place in your life where you can truly say, "This is enough!" This can be a painful experience but it is a powerful experience you can use to achieve your dreams. There are four basic stages in the process:

Disgust- When you get to place where you are disgusted with where you are, you say "That's it!" You have reached a point of no return, and you are ready to do whatever it takes to change. The gauntlet has been thrown down.

This happened in my life when I had been stuck in the same circumstances day in and day out for years. I was a slave to my low paying job, working in a position that I hated. I was driving a car I didn't want drive and I never had money to buy anything I wanted. There was no end in sight. I came to a point where I said "Enough!" and this was the day that I decided to change.

The Decision- After the initial stage of disgust, there is the point where you must decide which path you must take. There could be a multitude of paths before you, but now is the time to decide which one. Remember, action is what's important here. Don't spend so much time deciding on the path that you never move. It is better to choose the inferior decision than to never move at all. It's time to move.

Ambition- Another way to describe ambition can be desire. What causes some people to desire lofty excellent things, and others to be content with mediocrity? I don't know, but it's important to find out whatever that is for you. This desire can be initiated by anything. A poignant quote, a touching song, or meeting someone who has achieved your goals. Be on the alert for the trigger that turns on your ambition. Believe that you can achieve it. Embrace the experiences that can awaken the giant of ambition within.

Resolution- This is the final stage in process. This is the moment when you commit to never being the same again. You *resolve* that your goal will be achieved no matter what. A good way to frame this idea is to ask, "How long will I work on my goals?" The answer is, "Until I achieve them." This is the kind of resolve that allows men and women to overcome the most incredible circumstances imaginable. Humans are the only creatures that will settle for less than they are capable. I believe it is the double edged sword of human reason. Whenever you dig down deep and vow to yourself that you will win or die trying.

This may sound dramatic, but for this type of change to occur you need dramatic emotion to stir you up. Write it down. Make it a dramatic and memorable moment. Make this something that will fuel you when the going gets tough. Resolve to work as long as it takes!

Chapter 5

Find a Hero and Follow Them

Personal experience is a very valuable thing, especially in the western world. The problem, however, with personal experience is that it can be very expensive. Personal experience can be painful, and it can also require a large time investment. Something that is better than personal experience is learning from another's experience. Following a role model can save you years of trial and error, as well as immense pain and stress. There are men and women who have accomplished incredible things and offer to coach other people who want to do the same. These same successful men and women have written books or recorded audio on exactly how they achieved their dreams. It's an incredible resource to be able to follow the lead of these individuals, and skip many of the painful aspects of personal experience.

When choosing a hero or role model, remember the following things:

Pick a role model that has accomplished your dream.

Do some research, there have been men and women who have accomplished anything you can imagine. These people are all over the place, and lucky for us they offer to tell us how they did it. Remember not to over analyze this. Pick one that is close enough and go with them. Perfection is just the target; we must pick the best of the available options.

Mix the clay.

Listen to what this person has to say. Now is the time to listen. Learn the ins and outs, and soak up every detail. Capture the things that don't' really seem important or relevant to you at this time. Remember you are seeking the counsel of this individual. You don't know what is useful and what is not. Don't try to be so clever that you miss out on the useful information. Soak it all in. This is the clay that will turn into bricks. These bricks will be used to build your plan.

Write down the well-defined plan.

After the data is collected and you've gathered all of the information the role model has provided, begin to formulate your game plan. Review the game plan provided by the role model and tweak and adjust as you see fit. Be careful not the change the essentials of the plan. Remember you are following the role model. They have done most of the heavy lifting for you. You are learning in days and weeks what might have taken them 25 years to learn.

Commit to the plan.

One of the negative effects of there being such a multitude of resources available is that people are hesitant to commit to a plan in fear of missing out on a better opportunity. Many people have a perfectly fine plan before them, and if they would just execute it, they would be much further along than they are. Is it the absolute most optimal plan available? Probably not. But a decent plan executed is better than the perfect plan never executed. Commit to the plan in front of you with laser like focus.

If you commit to two months on a plan, and then realize after the time is up that you need another plan, then so be it. Most of the time, however, this will not be the case. A lot of action can make a decent plan produce great results. Remember, the perfect plan unexecuted is useless. Pick a plan and commit.

Chapter 6

Massive Action: Getting Down to It

We've covered a variety of topics so far in the book, but I wanted to end on a topic that I feel is the X factor for a successful life. Without this ingredient we cannot achieve even the smallest of goals. With this ingredient, our lives can be utterly transformed in every way imaginable. This ingredient is action, and specifically massive action.

We hear about motivation, we hear about preparation, we hear about all sorts of philosophies, but rarely do we hear someone tell us to roll up our sleeves and get to work. There is a time to philosophize and speak about theoreticals and motivation, but eventually we must act to see our dreams realized.

There really is only one secret to massive action:

Act Now - One of the problems with ambition is that if it's not promptly executed, the desire will fade away like a distant memory. Anyone who has had a desire and failed to act knows exactly what I am talking about. No matter how grand or how genuine your desires or intentions are, if they are not fanned like a fire they will go out. This is called the law of diminishing intent. The longer you wait to act on your intentions, the weaker they become until they dissolve into nothing. The road to failure is lined with discarded hope and grand intentions.

Remember: There will be no perfect time to act. Someone once said, "The best time to plant a tree was

20 years ago, the second best time is now." There are always reasons for not doing something. The result of a good reason and a bad reason are exactly the same- a goal unachieved. Today is the day that you start your journey on the road to your dreams. Stop waiting for someone to rile you up, and get you excited and ready to

work on your designed life. What are you going to do if they don't show up?

   Everyone hopes things will get better, but few experience their lives being transformed. Mere hoping will not change your life, no matter how strong it is. You must stoke your desire until it surfaces, and then act on it before it escapes. The first step of action is the beginning of the journey. That first step will create momentum and before you know it you are half way there. The time to act is now. If there is something you want to start, or know that you should do, go out and do it now. Whatever action is possible to execute today, do it. If you are truly interested in becoming successful you need to make action a habit. Procrastination is the profession of failures. Act now!

Conclusion

Thank you again for downloading this book!

I hope this book was able to help you begin the process of changing your thoughts, which will result in changing your life.

Remember your thoughts will create your reality. Make sure you are using your thoughts to help design the life that you want. The next step is to implement and practice these steps until they become a natural part of you. Remember, repetition is the architect of skill.

If you learned nothing else from this book, I hope you learned that you need to act on your desire. When you get that project idea or you feel motivated about that business plan, turn off your mind and act. An inferior plan with massive action is better than a perfect plan with no action. Whatever it is, now is the time to ACT!

Finally, if you enjoyed this book, then I'd like to ask you for a favor, would you be kind enough to leave a review for this book on Amazon? It'd be greatly appreciated!

Click here to leave a review for this book on Amazon!

Thank you and Good Luck!

www.ingramcontent.com/pod-product-compliance
Lightning Source LLC
Chambersburg PA
CBHW071019290526
45795CB00005B/1863